MY PET

HAMSTER

Nigel Taylor T.V. Vet

Cartoons by Mike Gordon

Illustrations by John Yates

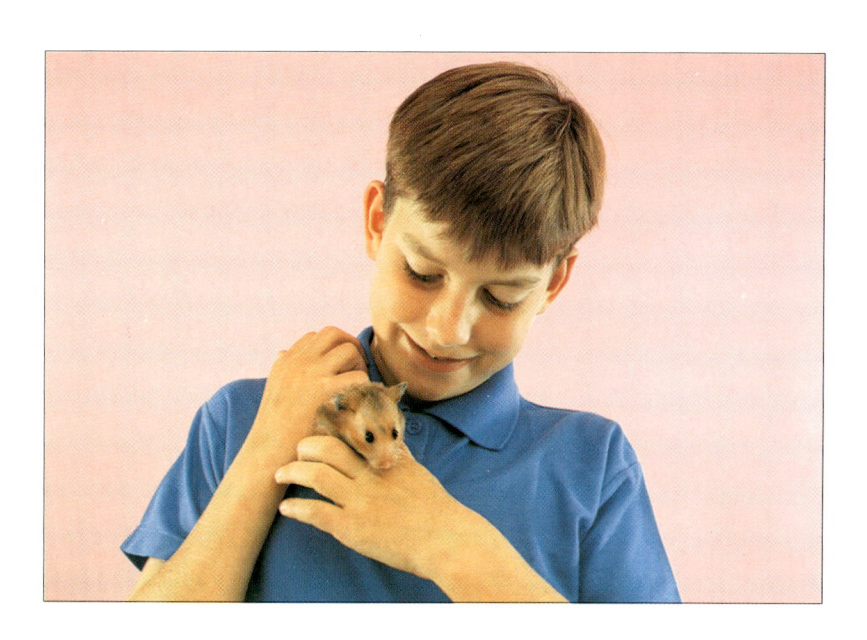

Wayland

MY PET

Titles in this series

Cat	Hamster
Dog	Mini Pets
Fish	Pony and Horse
Guinea Pig	Rabbit

To Michael and Cathryn

Title page Hamsters, like this
Golden hamster, make good pets.
They are usually friendly and easily
tamed.

Words in **bold** appear in the glossary.

Series editor: Geraldine Purcell
Designer: Jean Wheeler

© Copyright 1992 Wayland (Publishers) Ltd

First published in 1992 by Wayland (Publishers) Ltd,
61 Western Road, Hove, East Sussex, BN3 1JD, England

British Library Cataloguing in Publication Data
Taylor, Nigel
My pet hamster
I. Title
636.93233

HARDBACK ISBN 0-7502-0312-9

PAPERBACK ISBN 0-7502-0927-5

Typeset by Dorchester Typesetting Group Ltd, Dorchester
Printed by G. Canale & C.S.p.A., Turin

CONTENTS

Introduction

I am a great hamster fan. In fact, I think the hamster is one of the best pets for children there is. They are cheap to buy, clean and easy to look after. Most parents like them too, which is very important because owning a pet is very much a family responsibility. Hamsters are gentle, kind animals that respond well to careful handling and are usually easily **tamed**.

As pet hamsters live in cages, it is important that you are prepared to look after them well. You see, they cannot just pop down to the shops when they are feeling hungry or thirsty.

Opposite top All hamsters respond to gentle handling and affection.

You have to make sure they have fresh food and water *every* day for as long as they live, which is about two years.

Caring for your pet hamster will teach you a lot about living creatures, especially how well all animals respond to lots of love and affection.

Opposite far right Hamsters are lively and friendly animals when they are awake but they do like to sleep during the day.

Hamster record
You could keep a diary or record of your hamster's development. Keep a note of some of the following.
- Weight.
- When your hamster eats.
- Favourite foods.
- Sleeping patterns.
- When your hamster is active.
- Any visits to the vet and the advice given.

Not only will this record be interesting to look back on but it may also be used as a basis for a school science project.

Hamsters in the wild

Left A Golden hamster in its natural, desert home. In the hot, dry deserts hamsters have to search for food during the night, when it is cooler.

Hamsters are really desert dwellers. In fact, long ago everyone thought that Golden (or Syrian) hamsters were a bit like dinosaurs – extinct! Then, in 1930, a mother hamster and her babies (called pups) were found in a desert burrow in Syria. From just these few hamsters are descended all the many thousands, if not millions, of Golden hamsters there are in the world today.

Because hamsters normally live in the desert, it is not surprising that they spend most of the day asleep, as that is when it is very hot. Hamsters are more active at night. In fact, in the wild they run for many miles collecting the dry seeds and few plants that make up their desert diet. They tuck their food away in their **cheek pouches** and hurry back home before dawn. This is why your pet will be most active in the evenings and that is when you will see it at play and using up all its energy.

Below Hamsters enjoy their food. They can store a large amount of food in their cheek pouches.

Desert nights are very cold, so it is a good job hamsters have a warm fur coat to stop them from freezing while they are out hunting for food.

As they spend so much time in the dark, most hamsters are short-sighted and rely on their sense of smell much more than on their eyesight. If they wanted to see as well as humans they would have to wear glasses!

Hamsters like to live alone when they become adults. In the wild they only seek out other hamsters for **mating**. Two adult hamsters living together will often have punch-ups, so it is best to keep your pet on its own.

Below Golden hamsters often fight with each other, so if you don't keep them separated you will have bruised and battered hamsters!

Choosing your hamster

Hamsters have great personalities. Most of them are cheeky and, like you and your friends, a little bit naughty from time to time. They respond well to loving, caring owners. They are easy to look after, but they do rely on you, their owners, to feed them *every* day and keep their cages clean. Most well-cared-for hamsters live until they are about two years old. Males live a little bit longer than females but nobody knows why. Hamsters are very healthy animals whose behaviour is highly entertaining to watch.

Many owners buy their hamsters from pet shops. They are quite cheap and the most common variety is the Golden hamster. Not all Golden hamsters are gold in colour though. There is a terrific variety of hamster coat colours and markings.

Opposite This is a handsome looking European hamster. Its sparkling eyes and shiny coat show you how healthy it is.

Left It is important that you take your time when choosing a pet hamster. Make sure the one you choose is as healthy as this Golden hamster by reading the information box on page 12.

Hamsters with a single coat colour are known as 'selfs'. All hamster **breeders** hope to breed the Black 'self', an all black hamster which no one has bred yet. Each different coloured 'self' hamster is a recognized variety. These are further divided by ear or eye colour, for example the Cream, black-eared hamster.

Some hamsters have multicoloured or patterned coats. Then there are the banded hamsters with a broad white band around their middles. I think that the Tortoiseshell and White hamsters are very attractive.

All these varieties can each come with three types of fur. If you want to be a hairdresser later in life, why not try a long-haired hamster? These need plenty of daily **grooming** or else your hamster soon becomes a punk look-a-like!

Right It takes a lot of grooming to keep this long-haired Cinnamon and White hamster looking smart. Gentle, daily brushing will soon get your long-haired hamster used to all the hairdressing it will need.

For an extra-soft hamster there are always the lovely satins with their glossy, silky coats. Finally, there are the rex types with their close-cropped fur which feels like velvet.

The Russian hamster is also a very popular pet. These little animals come from Russia, Mongolia and parts of China. They are friendly, lively characters and, unlike the Golden hamster, can sometimes be kept in pairs.

Left Satin hamsters have shiny coats that are lovely to look at and soft to touch.

Below Rex hamsters have soft, crinkly, short fur which makes them look quite unusual.

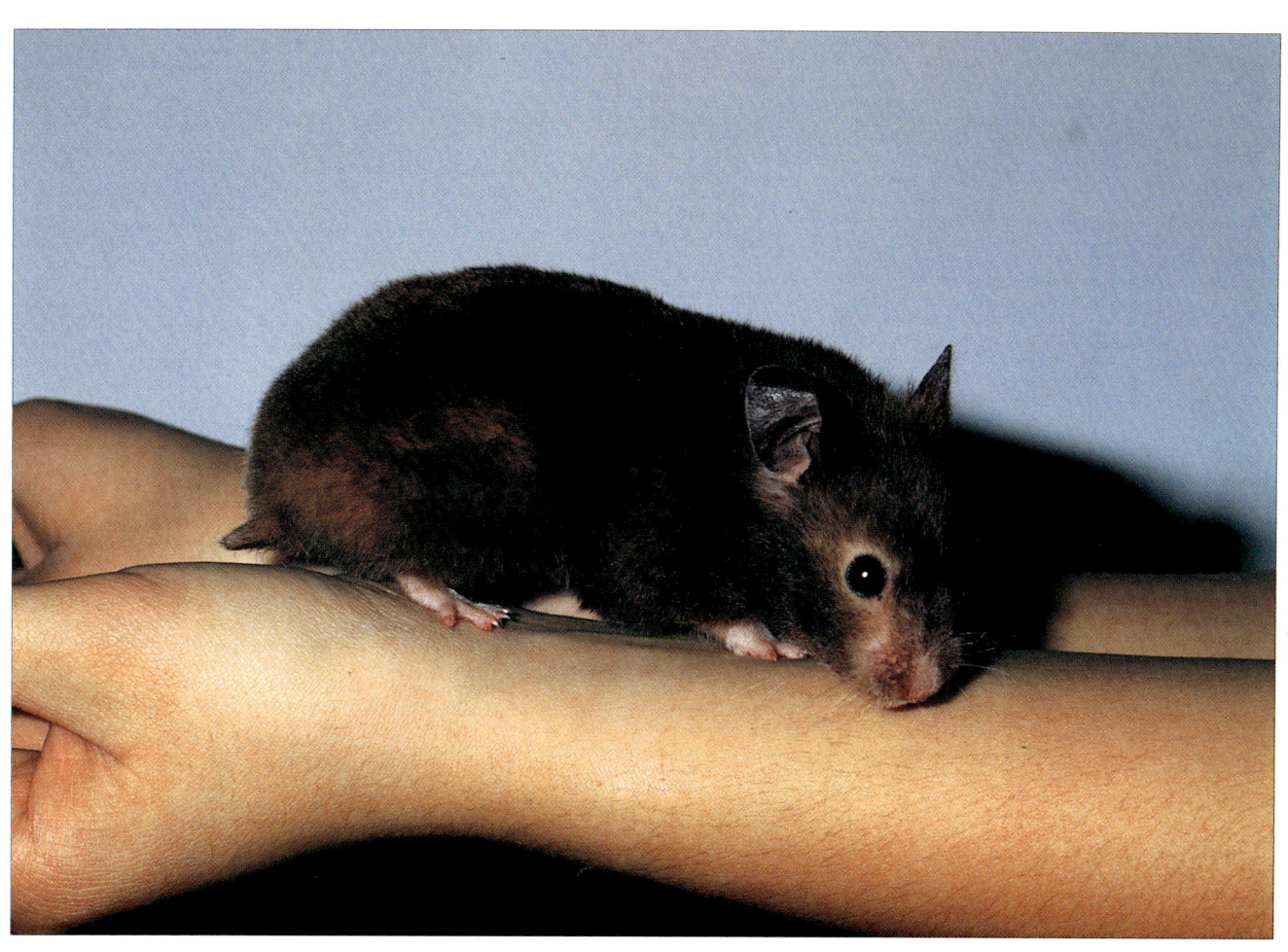

Left The Chinese hamster is very attractive but the females can be quite aggressive.

There is also the Chinese hamster. These have not proved so popular as family pets because the females can be highly aggressive.

So there you are, a great choice. Always buy healthy, lively hamsters from a good pet shop or breeder and you should not have too many problems.

If you are really interested in all the different types of hamsters there are, why not join a club for hamster owners? Your vet should know of a good club. Most clubs print newsletters which give advice and information. The club may even hold hamster shows – and you never know, you might own a champion!

Signs of a healthy hamster

Appetite	Eating well when active.
Coat	Clean and dry, not wet under the tail.
Mouth	Clean, no discharge.
Eyes	Bright and clear.
Nose	No discharge.
Pouches	Not swollen or sore.
Teeth	Clean, undamaged front teeth. Not overgrown.
Claws	Short, no splits.
Activity	Lively, burrowing and climbing.
Breathing	Quiet and regular.

A home for your hamster

Just like you, a hamster needs a comfortable home in which it can live safely and securely.

I like the plastic hamster skyscrapers you can buy at the pet shop. They are often called 'Rotastacks' and hamsters love them. You can build huge hamster space stations, connected up with all sorts of exciting tunnels for your pet to explore. I am sure all hamsters think they are Indiana Jones because they are always burrowing about, searching for adventure. Be careful though if your hamster gets too fat as I have heard of tubby hamsters getting stuck in the tunnels. Rotastacks are fairly easy to clean and, because they are mostly made of clear plastic, you can always see your hamster at play.

You might prefer a more traditional type of pet cage. You can buy a good-sized metal cage from

Left You should keep your hamster's cage clean and tidy because most hamsters are not very good 'house-keepers'.

13

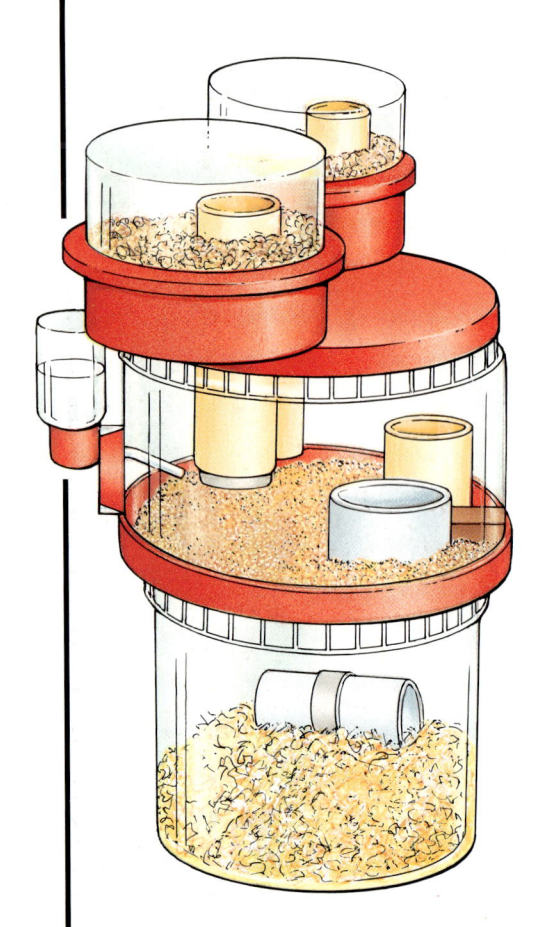

the pet shop. Remember, hamsters are great gnawers and will soon chew through wood, so metal cages are always that bit safer. Some hamster owners who are good at do-it-yourself make their own elaborate hamster homes with all sorts of burrows and tunnels. This sounds like a lot of hard work to me, and first-time hamster owners would probably find it a lot easier to buy a ready-made cage from the pet shop.

Whatever type of cage your hamster has, it will need cleaning at least once a week. Most people use sawdust to cover the cage floor as it soaks up any **urine**. Every day you must clean out all the hamster's droppings and damp sawdust you find in the cage. Some hamsters are really tidy and house-proud, but others are just like human teenagers and do not know how to keep their rooms clean!

Above Rotastacks are very popular with hamster owners. The great thing about them is that you can buy the main area first and then gradually add to it. This way your hamster has more and more room to play in and will not get too bored!

Right Rotastacks and metal cages are quite easy to clean. When you are replacing the bedding make sure you use safe materials, such as sawdust and hamster bedding from the pet shop. Never use cotton wool.

Above Happy hamsters snooze a lot during the day. This is because they are very active in the evenings and during the night.

Hamsters like to nest, so you must give yours some bedding to build its nest with. A nesting box in its cage is also a good idea. Shredded paper is quite good for nest building and so is the special hamster bedding you can buy at the pet shop. Try not to use paper with ink on it and never give your hamster cotton wool as this can kill them if it is swallowed. Some people like to use hay and wood shavings. Whatever you use, do not use too much of it. Most first-time hamster owners overdo the bedding and the sawdust so that the poor hamster can hardly move about in its cage.

Do not forget to keep your hamster's cage out of cold draughts and remember that they have sensitive hearing. Ghetto blasters and hamsters do not mix, so do not blast your poor hamster's eardrums with your favourite pop records by keeping its cage too near the radio.

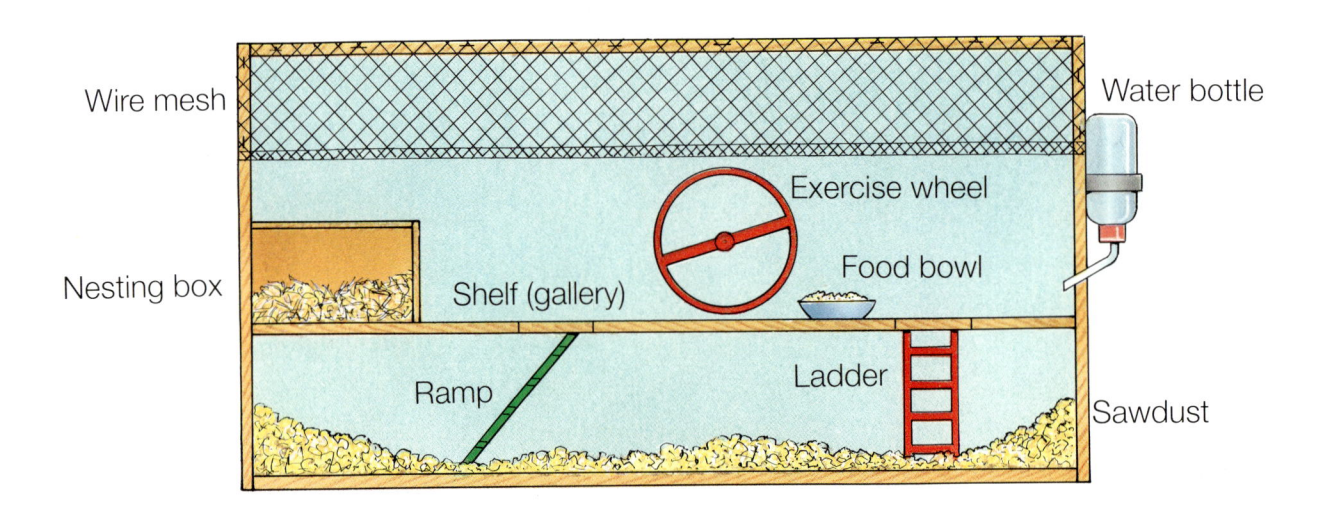

Clear, plastic top

Wire mesh

Water bottle

Exercise wheel

Food bowl

Nesting box

Shelf (gallery)

Ramp

Ladder

Sawdust

Above Hamster habitats are great fun to build – if you are good at woodwork! Hamsters like them because they are much bigger than the usual cages. In a properly made habitat, hamsters behave as they would in the wild.

D.I.Y. hamster habitat

The **R.S.P.C.A.** recommends that a hamster's **habitat** should be at least 75 cm x 40 cm x 40 cm. Make your habitat out of hardwood or softwood with a laminated (plastic) finish, for example Formica. Remember that any wooden framework left exposed will be gnawed by the hamster and damaged.

There should be a securely-fixed section of fine wire mesh running along the length of one side of the habitat. The height of the wire mesh should be around a quarter of the height of the habitat, that is 10 cm. The wire mesh section is very important as this allows fresh air into the habitat.

Fix a shelf or gallery about one-third of the way up the cage. The shelf has to be wide enough to contain the hamster's nesting area or box, exercise wheel, **drip-feed bottle** and food bowls. The hamster must have room to move around on the gallery as well. Then fix one or two ramps leading down to the burrowing basement you have created.

On this shelf level fix a solid exercise wheel to the wall of the habitat, making sure that it can turn freely but does not leave enough space for your hamster to crawl behind.

Put a layer of sawdust into the burrowing basement to absorb any urine. Hamsters usually use just one corner to urinate in. Keep this area clean and remove the hamster's droppings daily. Putting a small plastic tray into the corner helps with this job.

You need to check the habitat regularly to take out old food and to put fresh water into the water bottle daily. From time to time the whole habitat will have to be cleaned out and fresh sawdust and bedding put in.

Clean cages

Every day:

- Check your hamster's cage or habitat to remove any droppings, wet sawdust or old food.
- Give your hamster fresh food and refill the water bottle.

Every week:

- Completely clean out your hamster's cage or habitat.
- Remove all the old bedding and wash the base of the cage.
- Put in fresh bedding.

When cleaning out its cage make sure your hamster is safely in another secure cage or box with air-holes.

Feeding your hamster

Hamsters are easy to feed. They need a selection of cereal seeds, such as crushed oats, flaked maize, barley and wheat seeds for energy. You can buy pre-mixed seeds, grains and nuts from the pet shop. A few sunflower seeds and fresh peanuts, in moderation, are also good for them. Put this sort of dry food into earthenware bowls as your hamster will tip over or chew any other sort.

Below Healthy hamsters have big appetites.

Hamsters also like small amounts of fresh vegetables, such as carrots and cabbages, as well as fresh fruit. Apples, pears and tomatoes are real hamster delights.

Some hamsters like cheese and pieces of hard-boiled egg. Do not overdo these treats and make sure your hamster has fresh water from a drip-feed bottle every day.

Hamsters are great hoarders of food. In fact that is how they got their name – from the German word meaning 'to hoard'. Hamsters do not eat all their food at once. They fill their cheek pouches and store their food in a particular place in their cages or habitats to be eaten later. Do not overfeed your hamster as the uneaten food may go off which will make your hamster's cage very smelly. Remember that any animal that lives in a cage is totally reliant on you, its owner, to provide fresh food and water.

Below You should give your hamster a daily supply of various fresh fruits and vegetables.

Taming your hamster

You can start to tame your hamster soon after you bring it home. Start off by stroking it gently and gradually it will allow you to pick it up and hold it on your hand. Avoid sudden movements. Remember, sleepy hamsters do not like to be disturbed – they might bite first and ask questions later! Wait until your hamster is fully awake and active before you try to hold it.

With a lot of love and a little patience your hamster will soon be tamed and easy to hold. Some hamsters, like some people, are always a little bad-tempered I am afraid, so if your hamster is a hard nut, be careful!

Below left Let your hamster take its time getting used to your hand. Be patient and don't make sudden movements.

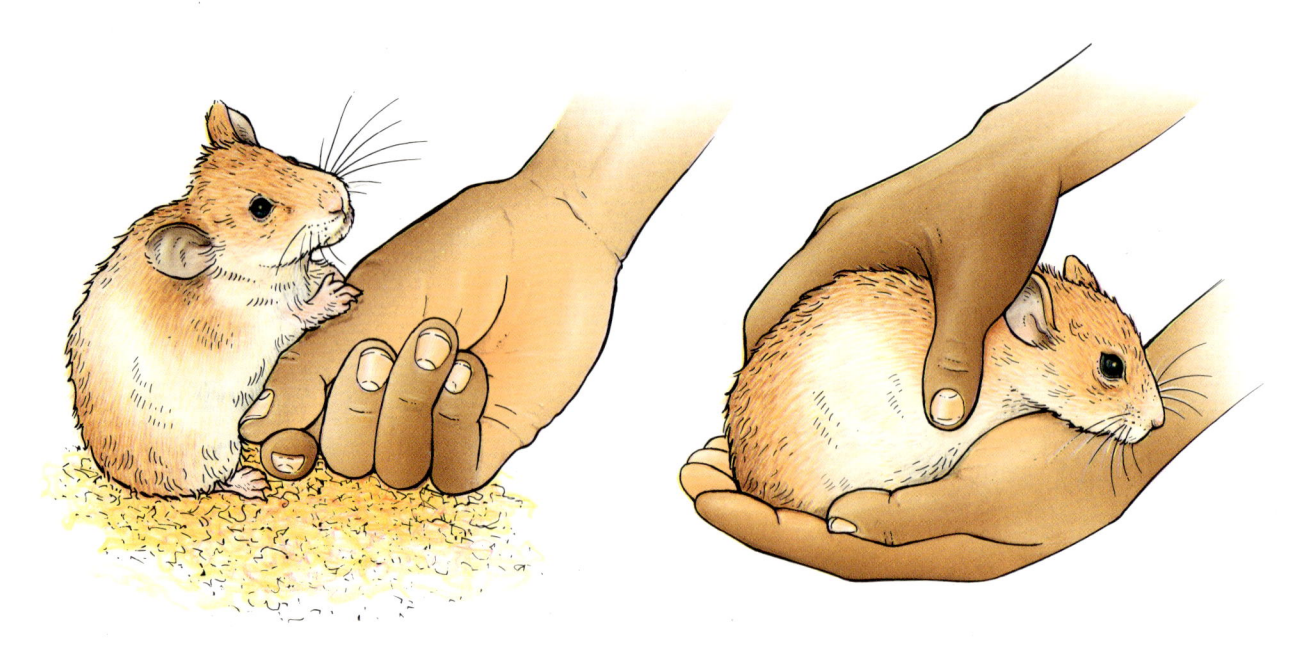

It is a good idea to get long-haired hamsters used to daily grooming fairly soon as otherwise their coat becomes matted and tangled. You can use an old, soft toothbrush, dampened with warm water, to groom your hamster.

Above When your hamster is confident let it climb into your open palm. Gently cup your other hand around your hamster to make it feel secure.

Hamsters at play

Hamsters are very active and they like to play a lot. Some owners, once their pet is tamed, like to let their hamsters roam about the house. Be careful though, because I once lost my hamster, Goldie, for a couple of weeks down the back of our sofa!

Hamsters soon get bored if there is nothing to do in their cages, so a few hamster toys to play with are important. The centres of old toilet rolls make great tunnels to crawl through. To keep your hamster busy and its teeth in trim you should put a chunk of wood into the cage for your hamster to gnaw.

Left Hamsters are great acrobats. They love to swing from the bars of their cages.

Handling hamsters

- Only try to pick up your hamster when it is awake.
- Coax your hamster into your hands. Do not grab at it.
- Do not put your hamster on its back, it will get upset.
- If your hamster is a bit fidgety, gently hold the scruff (loose flesh) on its neck.

Hamsters really like exercise wheels. Remember, in the desert they would travel for many kilometres each night so they have a lot of energy to use up. I treat a lot of hamster athletes with crushed toes who have had their feet caught in the rungs of open wheels. The best type of wheel is the solid plastic sort where there is no room for injury.

Below Hamsters enjoy their exercise wheels.

Breeding your hamster

Breeding pet hamsters takes a lot of care and experience, and for the first-time hamster owner it is probably not worth getting involved. But you might like to know how to tell the difference between male and female hamsters anyway. It is very simple – just take a look at the hamster's hindquarters. Females have rounded hindquarters. Males' hindquarters are tapered to a point and they have **penises**. As males become mature they also develop dark or black patches either side of their backs, just above their kidneys. These mark the position of their scent glands, which are used to attract a **mate**.

Mating

Female Golden hamsters are bigger than the male and they are able to breed at one month old. However, it is best to wait until the female is at least three months old.

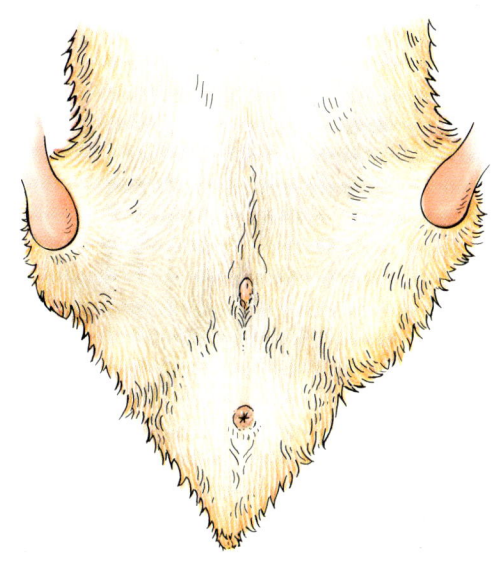

Above The male's genital area. The male's hindquarters are more pointed.

Below The female's genital area. The female's hindquarters are more rounded.

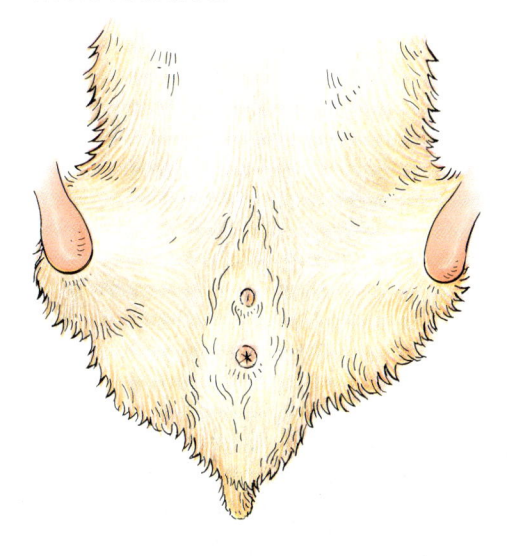

Left Once you are sure your pair of hamsters will not fight, then you can leave them alone to mate.

Always remember to bring the female to the male's cage and never the other way around. Hamsters can be very aggressive, even when mating, so you may have to separate them if they start to fight. You can always try again another day.

Pregnancy and young
Once the hamsters have mated, separate the pair immediately and return the female to her cage.

The female will be **pregnant** for about sixteen days. The average **litter** of pups – young hamsters – is between five and seven, but may be anything up to sixteen, so you should have new homes organized for as many as possible.

Baby hamsters are born blind and without fur or teeth. They must not be handled for at least sixteen days as they are far too delicate.

Do not disturb a nursing mother hamster as she can be very aggressive. If she is bothered too much the mother hamster may turn on her own young and kill them.

Extra food should be given to a pregnant and nursing female hamster. Wholemeal bread soaked in milk, fresh each day, is good for her.

Below If you leave your female hamster undisturbed she will keep her young pups safe and warm. If she is bothered, the female may become aggressive and hurt them.

The young will be **weaned** by three to four weeks old. They should be separated from the mother by the time they are four to five weeks old as she will begin to fight with them.

Soon after this the young male and female hamsters should be separated, and then they are ready to go to their new homes.

Left These hamster pups are two weeks old and are just starting to eat solid food as well as having their mum's milk.

Below Hamster families don't live together in the wild. So, when the pups are about one month old they should be separated from the mother and then taken to their new homes.

Keeping your hamster healthy

Hamsters are fairly healthy animals. It is important to remember though that you can do a lot to keep your hamster healthy just by keeping its cage clean and dry and feeding it a good balanced diet. There are some hamster illnesses you should know about as it is important to get your pet treated by a vet as soon as possible.

Wet tail
This unpleasant disease is caused by a digestive upset which leads to diarrhoea – very runny droppings. Cleaning the cage regularly and thoroughly will help prevent wet tail. If your

hamster looks dull and listless or has a wet patch beneath its tail, then take it to the vet. Many hamsters die from wet tail, so it is important to recognize the disease and have it treated.

Broken legs

Although your hamster looks like a cuddly toy, it is a living creature and does not like to be dropped from great heights! Too many tumbles and your hamster might end up with a broken leg or worse. Always handle your hamster gently and with care. Never leave them to run around on high surfaces, such as tables or sofas.

Losing fur

Lots of hamsters lose a bit of fur as they grow older, but if their skin becomes sore and itchy it means they have a skin infection. I often treat hamsters with ringworm (a fungal disease). This is easily prevented by keeping the cage clean and dry. As you can catch this fungus yourself, always make sure you wash your hands after handling a hamster with a skin problem. Your hamster should be treated by a vet.

Overgrown teeth

Sometimes hamsters' front teeth grow so long that they cannot eat any more. Your vet will clip them back to the right length so that your hamster can eat properly again. A wooden block to gnaw on in your hamster's cage is good at preventing this problem.

Sore eyes

Hamsters often get **conjunctivitis** which gives them itchy eyes. The vet will soon clear it up using special drops or an ointment. Get your pet treated as soon as you can.

Below Your hamster should be given something to gnaw on, such as a piece of wood, to keep its teeth in good health.

Sores and bites

Two hamsters living together often have punch-ups. Any bites can become infected, which may lead to an abscess – a pus-filled sore. If the bite or sore does not look too bad you can treat it with a mild antiseptic solution, such as watered down 'TCP' or 'Dettol'. If the sore looks nasty, go to the vet for proper treatment.

Hamsters sometimes get infections in their cheek pouches, especially if the wrong type of bedding is used in their cages. Always see a vet if your hamster's cheek pouches are swollen when they have not got food in them.

Hibernating hamsters

If it gets too cold, hamsters tend to hibernate which makes them appear to be in a coma or even dead. Don't panic! Moving the hamster's cage to a warm place, around 20°C, will usually be enough to revive it. Let it wake up gradually and do not disturb it too much.

Older hamsters are often quite dozy and frail. This is quite normal, but a little warmth and tender, loving care is a great help.

Coughs and sneezes

If you keep your hamster's cage in a draught, the hamster might well catch a cold, just like you would. If you do not watch out, the poor hamster may die of pneumonia – a chest infection. Dusty, damp cages can also make hamsters cough and splutter.

Your vet

Your vet knows a lot about hamsters and how they should be treated. If you are in any doubt or are worried about your hamster then have a chat with your vet. After all, he or she should be your hamster's best friend.

Glossary

Breeders People who keep male and female hamsters so that they can mate certain pairs together and produce young.

Cheek pouches On either side of a hamster's head and neck are loose pouches of skin which can store any food the hamster puts into its mouth but does not want to eat at that time.

Conjunctivitis An infection of the tissue around the eye which can cause swelling and soreness.

Drip-feed bottle A water bottle with a specially designed spout that only allows water to come through when an animal sucks at it.

Grooming The brushing or combing of an animal's coat so that it is kept clean.

Habitat The natural home, or a construction made to be like the natural home, of an animal.

Litter A family group of young hamsters (called pups).

Mate A partner of the opposite sex.

Mating When a male and female of a species of animal come together to produce young.

Penises The males' sexual organs used in the act of mating.

Pregnant When a female has mated and is carrying her unborn young inside her, she is pregnant.

R.S.P.C.A. The Royal Society for the Prevention of Cruelty to Animals. A leading British animal welfare organization.

Tamed When a young or wild animal becomes used to being handled and fed by a human.

Urine The liquid waste produced by animals when food and drink has been processed through the body.

Weaned When the young hamster's diet has changed from its mother's milk to normal adult food.

Further reading

For younger readers:
Care for your Hamster, by Tina Hearne (Collins, 1985)
Taking Care of your Hamster, by Joyce Pope (Franklin Watts, 1986)

For older readers:
The Going Live! Pet Book, by Nigel Taylor (BBC Books, 1989)

Hamsters, by J. Lawrence (Hamlyn, 1984)
Hamsters (Know Your Pet series), by Michael and Anna Sproule (Wayland, 1988)
Hamsters and Gerbils, by K. W. Smith (John Bartholomew, 1985)
A Petkeeper's Guide to Hamsters, by David Alderton (Salamander, 1985)
Pets for Keeps, by Dick King-Smith (Puffin Books, 1986)

Useful addresses

American Society for the Prevention of Cruelty to Animals (A.S.P.C.A.), 441 E. 92nd Street, New York, NY 10028, USA

Fur and Feather (fortnightly magazine), 1a East Cliff, Preston, Lancs. PR1 3JE, England

The Royal Society for the Prevention of Cruelty to Animals, The Manor House, Horsham, West Sussex RH12 1HG, England

Index

Picture acknowledgements

Animal Photography/(S A Thompson) 11 (top); Bruce Coleman Ltd/(J Burton) 10, 12, 21, 26/(H Reinhard) 8, 22; Oxford Scientific Films Ltd/(G I Bernard) 6 (top), (Z Leszczynski/Animals Animals) *cover*; Papilio 6 (bottom), 9, 11 (bottom), 13, 15, 18, 23, 25; WPL title page, 5, 14, 28.